MANAGEMENT: UP, DOWN AND INSIDE OUT

MANAGEMENT: UP, DOWN AND INSIDE OUT

(450 Practical Guides for Managerial Thought and Action)

By

M. Gene Newport

Professor of Management and Dean Emeritus
School of Business/Graduate School of Management
The University of Alabama at Birmingham

1stbooks - rev.01/20/00

ABOUT THE BOOK

Today's managers are covered up with things to read. Therefore, the appearance of another book on management usually receives little more than a polite yawn. Similarly, you probably think this one will give you nothing to write home about. But wait, this book is really different. How does it differ from all the others you haven't read yet? Read on and learn a little about it.

Above all, this look at management is short and to the point. It includes no pet theories, no survey results, no case analyses, and no quantitative data. In addition, you don't have to read it chapter by chapter. That's because there are no chapters. Instead, the book presents 450 short statements, each serving as a guide for managerial thought and action. This format lets you read as much, or as little, as you can stand at any one time.

The guides presented in this book will reinforce

many of your thoughts and actions, and they may take you in some new directions. Either way, you will see that virtually no facet of management has been left untouched. You will get some new ideas, experience lots of positive reinforcement, and find that you really can smile while reading a book on management. What could be better? Give this book a try and experience the fun of reading once again.

Preface

Today's managers are covered up with things to read. Numerous memos, letters, reports and e-mails arrive at their desks daily. Organizational training classes and self-development activities confront them with even more materials to be read. The net result is too much to read and too little time to do it.

After spending over 40 years as a professor of management, university administrator, and business consultant, I am well aware of the time constraints facing all managers. Therefore, this book was written to assist managers who want to explore the wealth of management concepts and guidelines now available, while helping them save time in the process.

The look at management included in this book is short and to the point. It includes no pet theories, no survey data, no new buzz words, and no "trendy" approaches telling you how to manage. You don't have to read it chapter by chapter, because there are no chapters. Instead, the book presents 450 short statements, all designed to serve as guides for managerial thought and action. This format lets you read as much, or as little, as your available time permits.

The 450 thought-provoking statements included for your reading pleasure will undoubtedly reinforce some of your own thoughts, observations and actions. In addition, they will probably take you in a few new directions. Either way, you will be exposed to some different ideas, experience lots of positive reinforcement, and find that reading another book about management really can be fun. What could be better?

M.G.N.
Birmingham, Alabama
October, 1999

1. Employees want to be led, not managed.

2. Successful managers learn to manage themselves first.

3. When other managers say they'll stand behind you, look over your shoulder periodically just to make sure.

4. Paying too much attention to the "bottom-line" can make you overlook other important items higher up on the page.

5. When you over-manage, you under-lead.

6. Achieving excellence requires a proper balance between management and leadership.

7. Mission statements can provide direction, but only actions produce results.

8. If you don't know where you're going, don't expect others to follow.

9. While other managers are saying, "it can't be done," look for ways to do it.

10. If placed in a situation where you might have to "fake it," leave the faking to someone else.

11. Admit your mistakes if you expect others to do the same.

12. Inaction is usually better than misdirected action.

13. If you don't know much about a topic being discussed, don't show it by opening your mouth.

14. If you want good advice, ask your employees.

15. Consultants who cost the most aren't necessarily the best.

16. Never belittle employees. Pride is one of their most important possessions.

17. Delegating is easy. Knowing when and to whom are the hard parts.

18. If opportunity knocks, have an open mind when you open the door.

19. Teaching old tricks to new managers doesn't result in progress.

20. Managers who rely on tight controls stifle employee creativity.

21. Continued self-development can keep you from becoming a missing link in your organization's chain-of-command.

22. The work of most committees would go faster if meetings were scheduled at 4:00 o'clock on Friday afternoons.

23. Fax machines seem to contribute to procrastination among some managers.

24. Tying managerial compensation to the results of employee opinion surveys might prove interesting.

25. Many managers start to fail when they first begin to misuse their authority.

26. The most effective managers spend more time listening than talking.

27. No organizational structure is either good or bad until people are added.

28. If money isn't a motivator, what has replaced it?

29. Trying to maintain the status-quo is a losing battle. An organization that isn't growing has already started to decline.

30.   Managers who talk the most in meetings do not necessarily make the greatest contributions.

31.   There is seldom a relationship between the length of a meeting and what is accomplished.

32.   Success is more likely when plans include input from those responsible for carrying them out.

33.   Implementing plans without provisions for control is like driving an automobile with no brakes.

34.   Knowing how to say no is as important as knowing when to say it.

35.   Knowing what takes place in the spaces between boxes on an organization chart is as important as understanding what goes on in the boxes.

36. No individual or group can accomplish anything without practicing management.

37. Employees are more motivated to accomplish organizational goals when they see that some of their own will be met in the process.

38. Reading the annual reports of some corporations is a sure cure for insomnia.

39. When you can't get the swamp drained because of the alligators, it's probably too late to try making friends with them.

40. Improve the management of its organizations and a nation's standard of living will increase dramatically.

41. Ethical behavior involves much more than adopting a code of ethics.

42. Total Quality Management requires total employee commitment and involvement.

43. When managers get big heads, they become smaller persons.

44. When you help another person learn, you both learn something.

45. Managers who spend their time reliving the past probably have no future.

46. Smiles, praise and courtesy are positive influences in all organizations.

47. Good managers focus on what's wrong, not who's wrong.

48. You won't be a winner if your behavior makes others question how you play the game.

49. You don't climb the corporate ladder by riding on an elevator.

50. Don't ask questions if you don't want to hear the answers.

51. Managers who are quick to blame others show their own faults in the process.

52. True corporate philanthropy responds to societal needs, not tax advantages or pet projects of key executives.

53. Remember employees' names and they will remember you.

54. Be careful when responding to critics. You may give them additional ammunition.

55. A plan without a vision is like a journey without a destination.

56. Managers who prefer dealing with the inconsequential shouldn't be surprised by the consequences.

57. Successful managers give instructions, not orders.

58. Focus decision making on eliminating problems, not their symptoms.

59. Even if you don't have a positive attitude, you don't have to be negative.

60. Managers who say something can't be done are often those who don't want to do it.

61. Your stress level is closely tied to how well you manage your time.

62. Employees can respect your position without respecting you.

63. The collective wisdom of an organization is the product of all employees, not just its managers.

64. Change will occur no matter how much you drag your feet.

65. Some managers believe they can, and they do. Others believe they can't, and they don't.

66. If you always deliver what you promise, you won't have to make as many promises.

67. Reading between the lines is important, but so is listening between the lines.

68. When employees think you are not interested in their problems, you have a problem.

69. When joining an organization, don't act as though nothing was ever accomplished before you got there.

70. Managers with big egos are on the road to becoming small persons.

71. Your body is your most important asset. Treat it accordingly.

72. Managers who develop their successors have met one of their most important responsibilities.

73. If you want something to remain confidential, don't tell it to others in confidence.

74. Wise managers don't praise employees privately and criticize them in public.

75. If all job candidates were as good as their resume's, hiring decisions would be much easier.

76. Those who have the most power in an organization do not necessarily have the most authority.

77. If first you don't succeed, try to find out why before trying again.

78. Few managers will be successful until they understand the politics of their organizations.

79. Asking for forgiveness rather than permission is usually a risky alternative.

30. Managers are judged by the company they keep, so choose your associates carefully.

31. Implementing controls too late is like having the family cat declawed after the furniture has been shredded.

32. Successful managers know that the future begins today, not tomorrow.

33. When two economists agree on anything, it's probably time to seek another opinion.

34. To some managers, an energy crisis means their employees are not working hard enough.

35. Depletion of natural resources is a major problem, but so is the underutilization of human resources.

36. Continued technological advancement requires the effective management of technology.

87. Many governmental regulations were brought about by managers who failed to regulate their own behavior.

88. Decision making can't be avoided, but you can choose to make the best possible decisions.

89. The future can't be predicted with certainty. Therefore, managers should always expect the unexpected.

90. Restructuring an organization will not necessarily change existing relationships between employees.

91. Effective working relationships between managers and employees are built on trust and mutual respect.

92. Never carry a soggy sandwich in a briefcase filled with important papers.

93. Leaders may be charismatic, but charisma is not leadership.

94.   The bottom line can't be changed by turning financial statements upside down.

95.   Just when you think you know everything, someone will ask a question you can't answer.

96.   The statement, "If it's not broken, don't try to fix it," has no meaning if you don't know whether or not it's broken.

97.   Managers who surround themselves with mediocre employees will take mediocrity to new heights.

98.   Pretending to be nice doesn't make you a nice person.

99.   Managers who commit to follow someone at all costs should at least try to estimate the costs first.

100.   Being #2 takes on a different meaning if you have only one competitor.

101. The problem with many staff managers is that they have never held line positions.

102. Managers searching for excellence should know what they are looking for before starting the search.

103. You are obviously disoriented if you don't know which end is up.

104. Teamwork suffers when a group's accomplishments are used for personal gain.

105. If you make a habit of mixing facts with opinions, you will ultimately be unable to tell the difference.

106. An organization staffed with perfectionists will never be good enough for any of them.

107. If managers stay focused on the worst that can happen, it usually will.

108. Actions are always better than good intentions.

09. If you like to give advice, you could probably use some yourself.

10. What you don't know is often what hurts your career the most.

11. Some managers see budgets as financial plans which exist to justify their overexpenditures.

12. It is easier to speak angry words than to eat them.

13. Many meetings would be shorter if the managers in attendance would close their mouths and open their minds.

14. Being conscientious and dragging your feet are two different things.

15. Doing something for the common good often requires uncommon managerial efforts.

116. Everybody wants to be somebody. If you help them, you will really be somebody.

117. Some jobs are so bad that employees actually feel better when they have to stay home sick.

118. When change seems overwhelming, managers should remember that it can only come one day at a time.

119. Phone calls, faxes and e-mails can save time, but face-to-face communication is still best in many situations.

120. A plan is no better than the assumptions used in its development.

121. The act of delegating does not give managers the right to meddle.

122. To some managers, a logical point of view is the one they express.

34

23. You grow wiser by learning from your mistakes. When you don't, you make a big mistake.

24. Many managers like strong nepotism policies because they don't want their children working for them.

25. About the time some managers see light at the end of the tunnel, their boss lengthens the tunnel.

26. Don't worry if you can't see the forest for the trees. Some managers can't see the trees.

27. Climbing a tree is one thing. Going out on a limb is another.

28. Always start your brain before engaging your mouth.

29. What you see in employees usually depends on what you're looking for.

130. Be wary of those who always start a conversation by asking if they can have just a minute of your time.

131. If you have doubts about doing something, maybe it shouldn't be done.

132. Making a name for yourself is often easier than keeping it.

133. Talking about all the work you have to do will not get it done.

134. Managers should never get too confident because a little self-doubt is a great motivator.

135. If you expect employees to check with you before making a decision, they will soon stop making decisions.

136. No wonder employees often feel insecure about the future. Things are bad enough for many of them right now.

37. Managers who like to talk about themselves usually don't want others to do likewise.

38. The best way to stop arguments is not to start them.

39. All managers acquire experience, but only wise ones learn from it.

40. Both corporate downsizing and dieting have the goal of eliminating excess weight.

41. Global warming won't help managers who vow to stay the course until hell freezes over.

42. Managers who go to great lengths to show how important they are, usually aren't.

43. Organizations can't compete if quality remains as nothing but a goal.

44. Managers who live in the past fail to prepare their organizations for the future.

145.	Plans are like maps. They provide routes to follow, but they can't eliminate detours.

146.	All organizations have an unidentified group of executives called "they." "They" want things done that others don't want to do. "They" issue policies that others don't like. And, "they" blame others when things go wrong. Strangely enough, though, many managers strive to become one of them.

147.	Don't let facts get in your way and you can make faster decisions. The quality of the decisions is, of course, open to question.

148.	If managers have to debate whether an action might be unethical, it probably will be.

149.	You can't think straight after you get angry, so do your thinking before you get that far.

150.	If it's so lonely at the top of an organization, why do managers work so hard to get there?

51. When faced with hiring someone only marginally qualified or not hiring at all, choose the latter.

52. Don't burden your organization with expenses you wouldn't want to pay yourself.

53. A few executives with large egos make an organization as top heavy as one with too many executives.

54. Those who manage by trial-and-error run the risk of making too many errors.

55. Managers who rely too heavily on statistics soon end up playing a numbers game.

56. Managers who cling to the tried and true often discover that something tried successfully in the past may no longer be true.

57. You won't see light at the end of the tunnel if you never enter the tunnel.

158. Managers are often faced with an identity crisis when the boss asks, "Who could have made such a stupid mistake?"

159. Mushrooms grow well when kept in the dark, but the same is not true for employees.

160. Like balloons, office rumors are inflated by a lot of hot air.

161. Being your own worst enemy may not be that bad when all other possibilities are considered.

162. Managers who don't know what they want should be prepared to take what they get.

163. To avoid feeling smug after being promoted, remember that what goes up must come down.

164. Developing the management abilities of others is like coaching an athletic team. You win some and you lose some.

65. Before you let a project pull you in over your head, make sure you know where the flotation devices are located.

66. Blowing your own horn sounds much better when you are part of an orchestra.

67. Going out on a limb is one thing. Staying there until someone saws it off is another.

68. When you're already in hot water, it's a little late to adjust the temperature.

69. Being prepared for the worst that can happen is a good way to prepare for the best.

70. Displaying self-confidence is good, but showing confidence in your employees is even better.

71. Letting unethical behavior go unnoticed is like leaving fish unrefrigerated. There will soon be a smell everyone will notice.

172. If you look before you leap, you may decide not to leap.

173. Dress like the boss, act like the boss, speak like the boss, and you'll still not be the boss.

174. Some employees trying to communicate with the boss feel like salmon swimming upstream with a hungry bear waiting to greet them.

175. Anything can be improved, but only if someone wants to do it.

176. Some managers thrive while others merely survive.

177. When addressing opposition, decide whether you are faced with differences of opinion or merely indifference.

178. When focused on a problem rather than personalities, differences of opinion can be very valuable.

79. Leading by example requires the ability to distinguish between good and bad examples.

80. Optimistic managers look for reasons to succeed while pessimists search for excuses to fail.

81. There is a big difference between managers who seek advice and those who depend on it.

82. It's a fact of life that change always brings some measure of sadness into management circles.

83. If you find a job easy the first time you do it, you may not be doing it right.

84. Making the same mistake twice is foolish. Expecting better results the second time is sheer stupidity.

85. Practice all you want, but sooner or later someone will start keeping score.

186. Managers tell people what to do while leaders motivate them to do it.

187. Managers who don't like to think are usually threatened by new ideas.

188. At the end of a hectic work week celebrate the fact that almost another 2 percent of the year is behind you.

189. The trouble with "golden parachutes" is that they don't open for all managers.

190. Trying to be like someone else is more acceptable than pretending to be someone else.

191. Managers remain responsible for those things they delegate to others.

192. If not much goes into planning the agenda for a meeting, not much will come out of it.

93. Managing by walking around does not include snooping around.

94. Board feet are found in a pile of lumber while bored feet can usually be found under a conference table.

95. Managers who like to tell employees where to go would already be there if wishes really came true.

96. Office rumors seldom contain all the facts. If they did, they wouldn't be as interesting.

97. Outspending competitors may work in the short run, but outsmarting them is a more lasting solution.

98. In the future, the "good old days" will be those facing managers today.

99. Measure personal success by your standards, not those used by other managers.

200. Wishing for change is no substitute for making it happen.

201. Some employees are thinkers and some are doers. Wise managers mix them together for the best results.

202. A trail of worry leads to uncertainty, selfishness, bitterness and sorrow for some managers.

203. Too many factions lead to less than desirable actions.

204. What some observers see as a meteoric rise to the top is more like a roller coaster ride to the managers involved.

205. If you need status symbols to show you've arrived, you haven't arrived.

206. Managers who complain about not getting dessert should make sure they've finished the main course.

07. The best preparation for some meetings is learning to yawn with your mouth closed.

08. If you can't remember what problem you were worrying about yesterday, it couldn't have been very important.

09. Sprinkling a lot of "you knows" throughout a conversation is, you know, very distracting, you know?

10. Both optimistic and pessimistic managers can be motivated, but motivation will take them in opposite directions.

11. Micromanagers typically see only small pieces of the "big picture."

12. Managers in their forties who start looking forward to retirement don't have much to look forward to.

13. Delegation doesn't relieve managers of their ultimate responsibility for results.

214. Some managers are content to wait for the future. Fortunately, others are eager to help create it.

215. Who managers know won't substitute for what they don't know.

216. Managers who try to outsmart their employees will often be outdumbed in return.

217. It's easier to get along with opinionated colleagues if you don't ask for their opinions.

218. If the grass looks greener elsewhere, check to make sure it's not artificial turf.

219. It doesn't help to cover your rear if competitors are launching a frontal attack.

220. You will never get on the fast track if the train doesn't stop at your station.

21. To some employees, laissez-faire managers are lazy, but fair.

22. Managers who expect to punt their way out of tight situations must first learn how to punt.

23. Judge job candidates by their knowledge, not just their education and experience.

24. Learning how to play the game doesn't mean learning how to bend the rules.

25. When my mother got her first sewing machine, she looked at it and said, "If only wishing would make it sew." Too many managers still say the same thing.

26. The trouble with a division of labor is that some employees don't like the way it's divided.

27. Never assume that success in one managerial position will guarantee equal success in another.

228. Managers operating at the break-even point are merely straddling the fence between profit and loss.

229. Managers either incur the costs of planning or the costs of failing to plan.

230. Managers who aren't willing to start at the bottom seldom make it to the top.

231. The goodbyes in some retirement speeches are so long they become lullabies.

232. Managers who blame predecessors for their problems are suffering from a form of PMS known as Prior Management Syndrome.

233. Pessimistic managers are so negative they are sometimes called no-nos.

234. Life-long learning keeps the deepest thoughts of managers from becoming shallow.

35. Managers who make mountains out of molehills will always have more mountains to climb.

36. If you don't know who's supposed to be in charge, better check to make sure it isn't you.

37. If your employees say they're caught between a rock and a hard place, make sure you aren't the hard place and then help them move the rock.

38. Managers who are self-confident find it easier to place their confidence in others.

39. Managers who look the best are those who look for the best in others.

40. Telling little white lies has started many managers on the road to telling some real whoppers.

41. Listen with your eyes open and what you see will often add to what you hear.

242. There would be no communication problems if people were not involved in the process.

243. Some managers don't know where they're going and some don't know where they've been. Funny thing, though, everyone is said to be proceeding according to plan.

244. When you're about to reach the end of your rope, better make sure a noose isn't waiting for you.

245. Managers who shoot from the lip are as dangerous as those who shoot from the hip.

246. Super managers don't waste time with the superficial.

247. Seeing yourself as other managers see you involves more than looking in a mirror.

248. Managers who spend too much time looking for the pot of gold will miss the beauty of the rainbow.

49. What you see in employees often determines what they see in you.

50. Managers who continually doubt the abilities of their employees usually find there is no rest for the wary.

51. A manager's road to success begins with high expectations.

52. Goals are like people. They come in all shapes and sizes, each with unique characteristics.

53. Excommunication isn't bad when it means your name has been removed from the circulation list for meaningless office memos.

54. Think before you speak. Words pass over your lips like water flowing over a dam, and once the flow has started it can't be reversed.

55. If you're not invited to all of the social functions hosted by your organization, be thankful.

256. Too little competition among employees can be bad, but so can too much. Seek the balance that encourages teamwork rather than individualism.

257. When managers around you are losing their heads, it's no time to stick out your neck.

258. When you are tempted to blame managers above you for certain problems, remember that those at lower levels are probably blaming you.

259. Some managers are so offensive that they become known as repeat offenders.

260. Managers who are too relentless run the risk of becoming unrelenting.

261. No manager's knowledge can equal the total of all group members.

262. Managers should measure for improvement, not to find fault or place blame.

63. A good leader does not have to be physically present to have an impact.

64. Successful managers know that the best time to search for improvements is when things are going well.

65. When managers become satisfied with the quality of products or services, they place their organizations at risk.

66. Wise managers know that good experience sometimes comes from bad judgment.

67. When seeking alternatives for dealing with change, avoiding it is not an option.

68. Putting the right person in the right job with the proper motivation is a primary responsibility of all managers.

69. The challenges of change can bring out the best that managers and employees have to offer.

270. Being a manager includes being a risk taker.

271. Good management starts with understanding what your organization is all about.

272. Don't rely on precedents to guide decision making, because what worked in the past may never be as effective when tried again.

273. Investing in self-development yields greater returns than many other investments.

274. If spending more money solved most problems, some organizations would have few problems other than bankruptcy.

275. Managers with positive attitudes can turn stumbling blocks into stepping stones.

276. Being up the creek without a paddle is better than being there without a boat.

277. An organization's vision is of no value unless it serves as a focal point for action.

78. All managers should remember that living it up is often hard to live down.

79. Bankruptcy can be caused by a shortage of ideas as well as a shortage of money.

80. Few things are truly lost until managers quit looking for them.

81. Managers don't gain recognition by calling attention to themselves.

82. Waiting for others to act sometimes becomes a big weight.

83. Managers who require a wake-up call to get started each day need to change either their sleeping habits or their jobs.

84. Managers should recognize that yielding to temptation is not an alternative to avoiding it.

285. Objections are often smokescreens, so wise managers look beyond the smoke and try to find the fire.

286. Unless getting dizzy is a manager's goal, running around in circles won't accomplish much.

287. Managers who are too busy to take a break should ask themselves if they have time for a breakdown.

288. Ideas that motivate can be entertaining, but they must also have meaning.

289. Customer complaints often provide opportunities when examined in detail.

290. Happy employees are not necessarily productive, and those who are productive are not necessarily happy.

291. Don't jump on the bandwagon until you know the executive leading the parade.

92. Managers become more creative when they stretch their imagination.

93. Young managers who become too bureaucratic run the risk of being called bureaubrats.

94. Putting employees on the hot seat often does little more than raise their temperatures to the boiling point.

95. Any definition of managerial perseverance can be summarized as, "keep trying."

96. Whatever your destination as a manager, you will never reach it until you undertake the journey.

97. Employees accept the fact that you'll feel down from time to time, but they won't accept you looking down on them.

98. It's hard to see the silver lining in a cloud if you're always looking down.

299. Managers with electric personalities can still find themselves without power.

300. For some managers success is relative, especially if the relative is a CEO.

301. Depending on the attitudes of other managers, being right can sometimes make you wrong.

302. Managers faced with choosing between what's right and what's wrong must first know the difference between them.

303. Listening helps managers broaden their outlook on problems.

304. Praise is hard to beat as a way to show your appreciation to employees.

305. Thoughtful managers don't treat employees thoughtlessly.

06. Indifference will not compensate for a manager's inability.

07. Accomplishment is often influenced more by the attitudes of managers than other organizational circumstances.

08. Employees develop greater self-confidence when managers listen to their views.

09. Managers determined to keep one foot in the past will never step forward into the future.

10. Don't offend others by asking for advice when you've already decided what you're going to do.

11. Employees always seem to listen better when you tell them something is confidential.

12. If all members of a committee agree on all issues, the committee is of little value.

313. Managers who aren't good at solving problems should at least try to avoid creating them.

314. It's hard for employees to take things with a grain of salt when they're being peppered with criticism.

315. When starting a new job, there is less time than you think to demonstrate your abilities, so get on with it.

316. Good advice depends on who is giving and who is receiving it.

317. Managers who follow the "me first" principle often come in last.

318. Many employees like to play matador when their boss becomes bull-headed.

319. Managers who blow their own horns too much are bound to hit some sour notes.

20. If worry hasn't advanced your career in management, work may be the answer.

21. Work that provides little enjoyment seldom provides long-lasting motivation.

22. Some managers talk so much they often get caught in their own mouth trap.

23. Managers who talk too much usually listen too little.

24. Managers who fight fire with fire often get burned in the process.

25. Managers who believe in winning at all costs are on the road to becoming losers.

26. Don't let yourself become known as a manager who asks the most questions, but has the fewest answers.

27. It does little good to set your sights high if you always shoot low.

328. Managers won't get anywhere by flapping their wings if they aren't willing to leave the nest.

329. If faced with choosing between two bad ideas, picking the best of the worst isn't a good alternative.

330. Negative attitudes lead to negative actions which produce negative results.

331. Wise managers do not abandon ship until the life boats are in the water.

332. Managers known as born losers are really potential winners who have given up.

333. The more risks managers take, the more they learn, and the more they learn, the fewer the risks.

334. Managers who aren't willing to carry the ball shouldn't expect others to run interference.

35. Rejecting another person's point of view is more acceptable if you have at least tried to understand it.

36. It may be better to not know where you're going than to not know where you are when you get there.

37. Optimistic managers look for the opportunities presented by problems while pessimists look for the problems presented by opportunities.

38. You will seldom see an employee's potential if you don't look for it.

39. It is unrealistic to assume that success as a manager can be achieved without some failures.

40. Having the last laugh doesn't mean employees won't direct a few giggles at you later.

341. Don't spend so much time getting organized that you don't have enough time to do anything else.

342. Managers who get out of the starting blocks first do not necessarily win the race.

343. Some employees are very pleased to learn that no two managers are alike.

344. There is a difference between taking a chance and taking a calculated risk.

345. Experienced managers know that a strong voice does not compensate for a weak argument.

346. It should not be assumed that managers in the twilight of their careers are operating in the dark.

347. Managers can learn from their mistakes, but they won't learn more by repeating them.

48. It sometimes seems that faster computers merely turn out more information that is used by fewer managers.

49. Approaching a situation with an ace in the hole is fine as long as you know what game you're playing.

50. Some managers will talk about their successes at the drop of a hat which explains why many employees have stopped wearing hats.

51. Managers can buy talented employees, but employee dedication is not for sale.

52. A sure way to end a conversation is to start talking about yourself.

53. Sooner or later, negative thoughts lead to negative words.

54. Some managers wait for a lucky break while others work hard and make their own luck.

355. Discussing the faults you see in employees is a sure way to point out your own.

356. Employee teams are motivated by challenges, not lip-service.

357. Training is an everyday responsibility of all managers.

358. Whether called challenges or opportunities, problems are still problems until some manager handles them.

359. Empowerment won't work very long if employees aren't permitted to make mistakes.

360. Some managers thrive on confrontation, perhaps because they are so confrontational themselves.

361. If managers prioritized the really important things in life, their jobs would be low on the list.

62. Successful managers keep employees motivated for the long haul, not just for today or tomorrow.

63. Few managers get lasting results through the sheer use of authority.

64. Slow and sure actions will beat fast and sloppy ones most of the time.

65. Leaders create work environments within which teamwork can flourish.

66. Effective managers serve as important links between innovative staff members and higher levels of management.

67. The good manager is also a good mentor.

68. A manager's personal integrity is built on more than words.

69. Managers who think an actuary is a home for birds will have trouble feathering their own nests.

70. Swimming with the current is not the same as being swept downstream.

71. Ignorance in action is the hallmark of some managers.

72. CYA memos often show more than they cover.

73. Managers who refuse to stand up and be counted are playing a numbers game.

74. If you look down on employees, your boss will soon be looking down on you.

75. Managers who cut too many corners end up going around in circles.

76. Only fools are sure of everything and that's why they are fools.

77. If you're appointed to a Committee on Committees, you've really arrived.

78. For everyone who praises your management abilities, there will be a long line of others waiting to voice their criticisms.

79. Committees can be valuable, but not when they destroy innovation and initiative.

80. Managers will never have time to smell the roses if they're always worried about the weeds in the garden.

81. Experienced managers know that hitting the ceiling only serves to damage your head.

82. Doing nothing doesn't leave much time for rest breaks.

83. Keep doing a little extra and you'll be known as an extraordinary manager.

84. Managers who do a job nearly right have still done it wrong.

85. Biting your tongue may be less painful than saying what you really feel.

86. Managers who deliver big don't have to make big promises.

87. If it's unethical, leave it undone.

88. The more managers know, the more they grow.

89. The best leaders in an organization are also the best followers.

90. Change makes some managers better and others bitter.

91. Leaders don't have to be physically present to have an impact.

92. Managers who change jobs too frequently risk becoming known as quick change artists.

93. Two birds in the bush may be worth more than one that messes in your hand.

94. Too many managers spend too much time avoiding obstacles that exist only in their minds.

95. Managers can work hard, double their salary, and still earn only half as much as they think they need.

96. Before you throw in the towel, make sure it isn't all you are wearing.

97. A dangerous combination includes some managers who don't know which end is up and others who don't know which way is up.

98. Don't worry if you are known as a manager who has made mistakes, unless you've made some really big ones.

99. In decision making, don't overlook the alternative of searching for more alternatives.

00. Knowing who's on first base may be relatively unimportant when all other variables are considered.

01. Some managers don't know where they're going, apparently thinking they can get there faster that way.

02. You have a big problem when you're self-employed and still don't like the boss.

03. Procrastination is just a matter of time for most managers.

04. Managers who don't want to do a job shouldn't consider delegation to be a reasonable alternative.

05. If something is not worth doing, managers shouldn't assume it will suddenly have value if they do it.

06. Give praise to employees and watch it multiply.

07. Trying to avoid doing something often requires more of a manager's time than doing it.

08. Being a part of change typically produces less anxiety than trying to stand apart from it.

09. There are times when playing dumb is better than trying to show how smart you are.

10. It's hard to believe, but some managers seem happiest when they are unhappy.

11. Some managers face too many deadlines that are self-imposed.

12. If you don't bark, you won't get caught barking up the wrong tree.

13. New managers should take a lesson from woodpeckers and use their head as much as possible.

14. Clothes can contribute to a manager's overall image, but it's what you have upstairs that still counts the most.

15. Small problems are sometimes made bigger by the managers attempting to solve them.

16. Searching for more data doesn't help managers strengthen a weak argument.

17. Don't assume that having "pull" means you can push employees around.

18. Managers who win by cheating are known as cheaters, not winners.

19. Don't expect problems to go away. Instead, get on with solving them.

20. Managers who are good communicators say the right things and then stop.

21. When you see light at the end of the tunnel, make sure it isn't coming your way.

22. Listen to older managers. They may not know more, but they've had more time to learn from their mistakes.

23. Being known for your character is not the same as being a character.

24. Being too wary can make managers weary.

25. Managers who are cautious optimists are close to being enthusiastic pessimists.

26. Managers who fail to delegate usually run out of solutions before running out of problems.

27. Accept employees for what they are, not what you'd like them to be.

28. When hiring employees, what you see is not always what you get.

29. When heads are rolling, it's no time to stick out your neck.

119

30. Employees are motivated by praise and deflated by criticism.

31. Leaving things to chance certainly limits your choices as a manager.

32. Some managers are managed by time. Others manage time.

33. Successful managers know that enthusiasm will sometimes substitute for logic.

34. The trouble with speaking from experience is that others may question your experience.

35. Doubt makes many managerial problems bigger than they really are.

36. Some managers use the past as a foundation while others try to make it the whole building.

37. Job knowledge and common sense make a good pair for any manager.

38. For many managers, luck seems to follow persistence.

39. The smartest managers are not always the wisest.

40. Employees don't resist all changes--just those they don't like.

41. Circling the wagons too soon can impede an organization's forward progress.

42. It's hard for managers to move forward while dragging their feet.

43. Managers can't soar with the eagles if they're squatting on the ground with the buzzards.

44. Opportunity knocks, but will not pick the lock for any manager.

45. Successful managers know when to stop preaching and start listening to their own sermons.

46. Managers who don't know which end is up, shouldn't look down.

47. Good luck flows from planning, perseverance and patience.

48. Some managers act and some think. A few rare ones do both.

49. Managers who can't look before they leap, shouldn't leap.

50. Many managers being bombarded with change are convinced that the future is not what it used to be.

ABOUT THE AUTHOR

M. Gene Newport holds a B.S. degree in Education om Eastern Illinois University. His M.S. in Management id Ph.D. in Business are from the University of Illinois. r. Newport has been active in higher education for some) years. Most recently, he completed over 22 years as ean, School of Business/Graduate School of anagement, The University of Alabama at Birmingham JAB), where he now serves as Professor of Management id Dean Emeritus.

Dr. Newport has provided consulting services for inks, insurance companies, educational institutions, ilities, construction firms, fast-food chains, hospitals, and vernmental agencies. In addition, Dr. Newport is the thor, co-author, or editor of seven books and has written imerous articles published in various business journals in e United States and abroad.